Annotated Teacher's Edition

. . . a resource of student activities
to accompany *Write Source*

WRITE SOURCE®

GREAT SOURCE EDUCATION GROUP
a Houghton Mifflin Company
Wilmington, Massachusetts

A Few Words About the
Write Away SkillsBook

Before you begin . . .

The *SkillsBook* provides you with opportunities to practice editing and proofreading skills presented in *Write Source*. The *Write Source* contains guidelines, examples, and models to help you complete your work in the *SkillsBook*.

Each *SkillsBook* activity includes a brief introduction to the topic and examples showing how to complete that activity. You will be directed to the page numbers in the *Write Source* for additional information and examples. The "Proofreading Activities" focus on punctuation, the mechanics of writing, usage, and spelling. The "Sentence Activities" provide practice in sentence combining and in correcting common sentence problems. The "Language Activities" highlight the parts of speech.

Many exercises end with a KEEP GOING activity. Its purpose is to provide follow-up work that will help you apply what you have learned in your own writing.

Authors: Pat Sebranek and Dave Kemper

Great Source and **Write Source** are registered trademarks of Houghton Mifflin Company.

Printed in the United States of America

International Standard Book Number: 0-669-51817-4 (student edition)

2 3 4 5 6 7 8 9 10 QWD 10 09 08 07

ISBN 13: 978-0-669-51822-1   I SBN 10: 0-669-51822-0

2 3 4 5 6 7 8 9 10 QWD 10 09 08 07

Table of Contents

Checking Mechanics

Using the Right Word

Sentence Activities

Language Activities

Proofreading Activities

The activities in this section include sentences that need to be checked for punctuation, mechanics, or usage. Most of the activities also include helpful *Write Source* references. In addition, KEEP GOING, which is at the end of many activities, encourages follow-up practice of certain skills.

Name

_____

Periods as End Punctuation

A **period** is used as a signal to stop at the end of a sentence. Put a period at the end of a telling sentence.

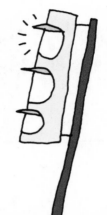

A   Put periods at the ends of these telling sentences.

1. Our class lines up at the main door ___.___

2. Sometimes we make our teacher smile ___.___

3. We play indoors on rainy days ___.___

4. There are some great new books in the library ___.___

5. I like to write funny stories ___.___

B   Write two telling sentences about your school.

1. _____

_____

2. _____

_____

C Put a period at the end of each sentence in this letter.

October 10, 2006

Dear Aunt Fran,

I like school this year. There are 22 kids in my class. A new boy sits next to me. His name is Robert. I think we're going to be friends. I'll let you know in my next letter.

Love,

Timmy

KEEP GOING

Now answer these questions about the letter.

1. How many telling sentences are in the letter? _____ 6

2. How many periods are in the letter? _____ 6

Name _____

Periods After Abbreviations

Use **periods** after these abbreviations:
Mr., Mrs., Ms., and Dr.

Dr. Green   Mrs. Linn

(**Dr.** is the abbreviation for **doctor**.)

A Put periods after the abbreviations in these sentences. (Some sentences need more than one period.)

1. Mrs. Linn is our teacher.

2. Mr. and Mrs. Linn have three rabbits.

3. Mr. Linn gave the rabbits their names.

4. They are Ms. Hop, Mr. Skip, and Mrs. Jump.

5. Mrs. Linn took the rabbits to Dr. Green for shots.

6. Dr. Green said, "Those are good names!"

7. Mrs. Linn told Dr. Green that Mr. Linn made up

the names.

6

B

Write two names for rabbits. One name should start with Mr. and one with Mrs. Then write two sentences that use the names.

Name: _Mr._ _____

Name: _Mrs._ _____

1. _____

_____

_____

2. _____

_____

_____

C

Write the names of four grown-ups. Be sure to write Mr., Mrs., Ms., or Dr. before each name.

1. _____

2. _____

3. _____

4. _____

Name _____

Question Marks

Put a **question mark** after a sentence that asks a question.

What is the longest river?

A Put a question mark after each sentence that asks a question. Put a period after each of the other sentences.

1. The world's longest river is the Nile ___•___

2. Where is the Nile ___?___

3. The Nile River is in Africa ___•___

4. Are there crocodiles in the Nile ___?___

5. You could jump in and find out ___•___

6. Are you kidding ___?___

7. I'd rather just ask someone ___•___

8. Are you afraid of crocodiles ___?___

9. Who wouldn't be afraid ___?___

B **Put a period or a question mark at the end of each sentence in this paragraph.**

Lots of animals live in rivers. Of course, fish live in rivers. What else lives in rivers? Snails, frogs, and turtles live in and around rivers. Have you heard of river otters? They are very good at diving. They can stay underwater for four minutes. Do you know any other animals that live in rivers?

Write two questions about rivers. Remember to use question marks!

1. _____

_____

2. _____

_____

Name _____

Exclamation Points

Put an **exclamation point** after an *excited* word. Also put an exclamation point after a sentence showing strong feeling.

Help!   Yikes!

Don't touch that!

A Use an exclamation point or period to finish each sentence. Remember, an exclamation point is used after each *excited* word and after each sentence that shows strong feeling. Telling sentences need a period.

1. I found a treasure map___!___

2. It was in my closet_____.____

3. I found the map when I cleaned my room_____.____

4. Wow____!____

5. Let's find the treasure_____!____

6. We should ask our parents before we look_____.____

7. This could be fun_____!____

B Each of the following sentences needs an exclamation point or a question mark. Put the correct end punctuation after each sentence.

1. Look, Tom, it's a cave _____!_____

2. It's dark _____!_____

3. It's creepy _____!_____

4. Did you see that _____?_____

5. What is it _____?_____

6. It's a bat _____!_____

7. Wow, that's neat _____!_____

8. Here we go _____!_____

Imagine that you are in a dark cave. Write a sentence that ends with an exclamation point.

_____

_____

Name _____

End Punctuation

Use a **period (.)** after a telling sentence. Use a **question mark (?)** after a sentence that asks a question. Use an **exclamation point (!)** after a sentence that shows strong feeling.

A **Put the correct end punctuation after each sentence.**

(Some answers may vary.)

1. Dad's taking us to the zoo ___!___

2. Hooray! Let's have a race to the car ___!___

3. What animal does Dad like ___?___

4. He likes the elephants ___.___

5. What do you think Mom wants to see ___?___

6. She'll probably watch the giraffes ___.___

7. What should we do ___?___

8. Let's go see the seals ___!___ (or) .

B Write a telling sentence, an asking sentence, and a sentence showing strong feeling about your favorite dinner.

Telling Sentence: _____

_____

Asking Sentence: _____

_____

Strong Feeling Sentence: _____

_____

C Ask a partner a question. Write your partner's name, the question you asked, and your partner's answer.

Partner's Name: _____

Question: _____

_____

Answer: _____

_____

Name _____

End Punctuation Review

Use a **period** after a telling sentence. Use a **question mark** after a sentence that asks a question. Use an **exclamation point** after a sentence that shows strong feeling.

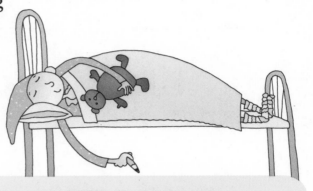

A **Put the correct end punctuation after each sentence.**

(Some answers will vary.)

Does this ever happen to you? It's time for bed, but you're not sleepy. You try to lie still. You look around. You just have to get up! You want to get a book or a toy. You try to be quiet. It's hard to see in the dark. You make a loud noise. Someone says, "What's going on in there?" Then you hear, "Get back in bed!"

B Draw a picture of something you like to do after school.

C Write three sentences about your picture. First write a telling sentence. Next write a question. Then write a sentence that shows strong feeling.

1. Telling Sentence:_____

_____

2. Asking Sentence:_____

_____

3. Strong Feeling Sentence: _____

_____

Name

_____

Commas Between Words in a Series

Put **commas** between words in a series.

The five senses are sight, hearing, taste, smell, and touch.

A Put commas where they are needed in these sentences.

1. Most foods taste sweet, sour, or salty.

2. Smell, sight, and taste help us enjoy food.

3. Almost everybody likes warm bread, biscuits, and dinner rolls.

4. Lilies, lilacs, and roses smell good.

5. Cats can see only black, white, and gray.

6. Dogs, cats, and bats hear all kinds of sounds.

7. Sounds can be loud, soft, or just right.

8. Teddy bears are soft, cuddly, and fuzzy.

B   List three or four things in each category below.

My Favorite **Tastes**	My Favorite **Smells**	My Favorite **Sounds**

C   Finish the sentences below using words from your lists. Remember to use commas between words in a series.

1. My favorite tastes are _____

_____ and _____ .

2. My favorite smells are _____

_____ and _____ .

3. My favorite sounds are _____

_____ and _____ .

Name _____

Commas in Compound Sentences

A **compound sentence** is two short sentences connected by *or*, *and*, or *but*. Always use a **comma** before the connecting word.

I have a goldfish, and I feed it once a day.

A Add a comma to each of these compound sentences.

1. I love hamburgers, but I do not like onions.

2. My brother is three, and he goes to preschool.

3. You can walk, or you can ride your bike.

4. Dad came to the concert, but Mom had to work.

5. Our teacher is nice, and she loves dogs.

6. Sara will play the piano, or she will sing.

7. I asked Lee to play ball, but he was busy.

B Write compound sentences using the pairs of sentences below. Use the connecting word in parentheses to complete each sentence. Remember to add commas!

Do you see the bees? Can you hear them? (or)
Do you see the bees, or can you hear them?

1. Bees are busy. They all have jobs to do. *(and)*

Bees are busy, and they all have jobs to do.

_____

_____

2. Most bees work. The queen bee does not work. *(but)*

Most bees work, but the queen bee does not work.

_____

_____

3. Bees care for the queen. They make honey. *(or)*

Bees care for the queen, or they make honey.

_____

_____

Name

Commas to Set Off a Speaker's Words

When you write a speaker's exact words, you may tell who is speaking at the **beginning** of the sentence, or at the **end** of the sentence. Use a comma to set off the speaker's words, as shown below.

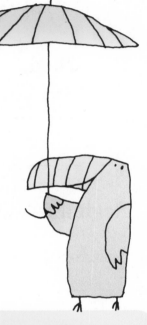

Mr. Kent said, "Kari, you may begin your report."

"My report is on birds," Kari said.

 **A** **Put commas where they are needed in these sentences.**

"Many birds migrate in the winter," Kari said.

Darrin asked, "What does *migrate* mean?"

"Migrate means that some birds go to a new place in winter," Kari answered. She added, "Birds migrate to find food and water."

"That's very interesting," said Mr. Kent.

B Write questions that Bill and Regina might ask about birds and migration. Use question marks and commas correctly.

Bill asked __ " _____

_____

_____ "

Regina asked __ " _____

_____

_____ "

List three places you would like to migrate (travel) to.

1. _____

2. _____

3. _____

Name
_____

Comma Between a City and a State

Put a **comma** between the name of a city and a state.

Austin **,** Texas   Salem **,** Oregon

 **A**   **Put commas between the cities and states below.**

1. Calumet **,** Michigan

2. Casper **,** Wyoming

3. Williamsburg **,** Virginia

4. Portland **,** Maine

5. Dallas **,** Texas

6. Dayton **,** Ohio

B   **Write the name of the city and state shown on page 388 in your *Write Source*. Then write the name of another city and its state. Put a comma between the city and state.**

1. _____

2. _____

Draw a picture of a place in your city or town. Beneath your drawing, write sentences about your picture.

I live in_____

_____

_____

_____

_____

Name

Comma Between the Day and the Year

Put a **comma** between the day and the year.

January 17, 2006
November 12, 2006

June 2006

S	M	T	W	T	F	S
				1	2	3
4	5	6	7	8	9	10
(11)	12	13	14	15	16	17
18	19	20	21	22	23	◇24◇
25	26	27	28	29	30	

A Look at the calendar on this page. Then write the correct month, day, and year.

1. Write the date that is circled.

June 11, 2006

2. Write the date that has a diamond around it.

June 24, 2006

3. Write the date for the last day of the month.

June 30, 2006

4. Write the date for the first Monday of the month.

June 5, 2006

B Write the dates for the following days. Be sure to include the month, day, and year. The months are listed on page 406 in *Write Source*.

1. Your next birthday:

_____

2. Today:

_____

3. Tomorrow:

_____

Write a true or make-believe sentence about the day you were born. Include the date of your birth in your sentence.

_____

_____

_____

_____

Name _____

Commas in Letters

Put **commas** after the greeting and
the closing of a letter.

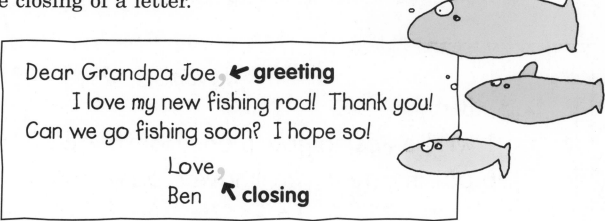

Dear Grandpa Joe, ← **greeting**
        I love my new fishing rod! Thank you!
Can we go fishing soon? I hope so!
                Love,
                Ben ↖ **closing**

A **Put commas where they belong in these letters.**

November 10, 2006
Dear Ben,
    Ask your mom
when your family is
coming to Florida.
Then we can go
fishing.
        Love,
        Grandpa Joe

November 18, 2006
Dear Grandpa Joe,
    We are coming to
see you on December
23. I can't wait! My
tackle box is ready.
        Love,
        Ben

B Put commas in Grandpa's letter. Then pretend you are Ben. Write what you would say in your next letter to Grandpa Joe. Be sure to put commas in the right places.

November 24, 2006

Dear Ben,
    I will be seeing you in one month! We'll camp out in a tent. We'll have a campfire.
        Love,
        Grandpa Joe

_____
(Date)

_____
(Greeting)

_____

_____

_____
(Closing)

_____
(Signature)

Name
_____

Comma Review

This activity reviews comma uses you have learned.

 **A** **Put a comma between the names of the cities and the states in these sentences.**

1. You can see mountains from Portland, Oregon.

2. The James River goes through Richmond, Virginia.

3. El Paso, Texas, is near Mexico.

4. Sitka, Alaska, is on the Pacific Ocean.

5. Hilo, Hawaii, is part of an island.

B **Put a comma between the day and the year in these sentences.**

1. George Washington was born February 22, 1732.

2. The first nickel was made on May 16, 1866.

3. On February 7, 1867, Laura Ingalls Wilder was born.

4. The astronaut Sally Ride was born May 26, 1951.

C Put commas between words in a series in these sentences.

1. Red, orange, yellow, and green are rainbow colors.

2. My uncle, aunt, and cousin live in Michigan.

3. Jonathan likes snowboarding, sledding, and skiing.

4. My family has two cats, one dog, and a turtle.

5. I send letters, notes, and e-mail messages.

D Put commas where they are needed.

Maggie asked, "What kind of seashell is that?"

"It's a heart cockle," Molly said. "If you put two together, they form a heart."

"Amazing!" Maggie added. "What's this one?"

"It's called a turkey wing," Molly answered.

"That's a perfect name! It looks just like one," said Maggie.

Name

_____

Making Contractions 1

A **contraction** turns two words into one word. To make a contraction, put an **apostrophe** where one or more letters are left out.

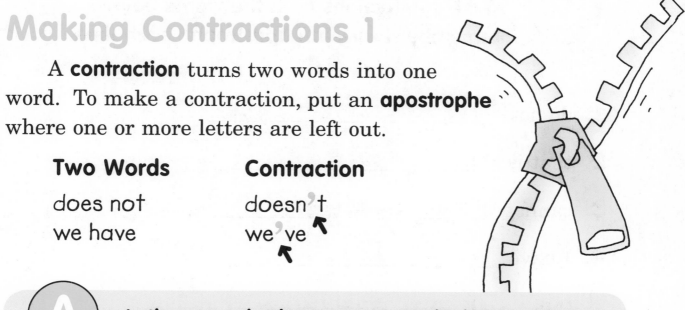

Two Words

does not
we have

Contraction

doesn't
we've

A   **In the second column, cross out the letters that are left out of the contraction in the first column.**

Contraction	Two Words
1. I'm	I am
2. she'll	she will
3. he's	he is
4. they're	they are
5. he'd	he would
6. hasn't	has not
7. we'll	we will
8. shouldn't	should not

B **Make contractions from the words below. Remember to use an apostrophe each time!**

1. do not _____ don't _____

2. that is _____ that's _____

3. cannot _____ can't _____

4. I have _____ I've _____

C **On each blank below, write the contraction for the words in parentheses.**

1. _____ I'm _____ going to make a mask.
      (I am)

2. _____ I'll _____ make it out of a paper bag.
      (I will)

3. _____ It's _____ going to be a scary mask.
      (It is)

4. Dad _____ doesn't _____ know I am making it.
      (does not)

Name
_____

Making Contractions 2

A **contraction** turns two words into one word. To make a contraction, put an **apostrophe** where one or more letters are left out.

Two Words	Contraction
she will	she'll

A — In each sentence, underline the contraction. Then write the word or words the contraction stands for.

1. "Peter <u>didn't</u> obey Mom," said Flopsy. ___did not___

2. "You can't go to the ball," she told Cinderella.

_____cannot_____

3. "You wouldn't help me," said the Little Red Hen.

_____would not_____

4. "I couldn't sleep in that bumpy bed," said the princess.

_____could not_____

5. The wolf said, "I'll blow your house down." ____I will____

6. "I'm a real boy!" shouted Pinocchio. ____I am____

B Write the two words that each contraction stands for.

1. doesn't _____does not_____

2. hasn't _____has not_____

3. he's _____he is_____

4. I've _____I have_____

5. isn't _____is not_____

6. it's _____it is_____

7. we're _____we are_____

8. you'll _____you will_____

Write a sentence using one of the contractions above.

_____

_____

_____

Name

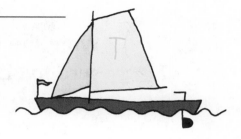

Apostrophes to Show Ownership

Add an **apostrophe** and an **s** to a word to show ownership.

Tom has a boat.   It is Tom's boat.

 **Each phrase below shows ownership. Draw a picture in each box.**

the cat's rug	the bird's nest
Susan's jump rope	my mother's hat

B Write the words below to show ownership. Be sure to add an apostrophe and an *s* to each word.

1. the _____tree's_____ leaves
   (tree)

2. the _____kite's_____ string
   (kite)

3. the _____airplane's_____ wing
   (airplane)

4. the _____bird's_____ tail
   (bird)

C Write the names below to show ownership. Add an apostrophe and an *s* to each name.

1. I see _____Maria's_____ purple pencil.
   (Maria)

2. This is _____Don's_____ math book.
   (Don)

3. _____Jane's_____ backpack is heavier than mine.
   (Jane)

4. _____Sol's_____ idea notebook is on the desk.
   (Sol)

Name _____

Underlining Titles

Underline the titles of books and magazines.

    a book — Onion Sundaes ↙

    a magazine — 3, 2, 1 Contact

A   **Underline the titles in the following sentences.**

1. My sister's favorite book is <u>Pocahontas</u>.

2. My grandmother has a book called <u>Mrs. Bird</u>.

3. <u>Kids Discover</u> is a magazine for kids.

4. The title of our book is <u>Write Source</u>.

5. <u>Ranger Rick</u> is a nature magazine for kids.

6. I just read <u>Ira Sleeps Over</u> by Bernard Waber.

7. My dad reads <u>National Geographic</u> every month.

8. Our teacher is reading <u>All About Sam</u> to us.

B **Complete the following sentences. Remember to underline the titles.**

1. My favorite book is _____

_____ .

2. My favorite magazine is _____

_____ .

3. The title of the last book I read is _____

_____ .

Draw a cover for one of your favorite books. Write the book title on your cover.

Name

Quotation Marks Before and After a Speaker's Words

Comic strips make it easy to tell who is speaking. They use speech balloons. Here Mom and Steve are talking about dinner.

When you write sentences, you use **quotation marks** to show the speaker's exact words.

Steve asked, "Mom, may we make pizza for dinner?"

"That sounds really good to me," Mom said.

A Read the speech balloons. Then write the sentences below. Put quotation marks where they are needed.

May we make pepperoni pizza?

Yes, Let's add something else.

Steve asked, _____"May we make pepperoni pizza?"_____

_____

Mom answered, _____"Yes. Let's add something else."_____

_____

How about mushrooms?

Great choice!

Steve asked, _____"How about mushrooms?"_____

_____

Mom said, _____"Great choice!"_____

_____

Name _____

Punctuation Review

This review covers punctuation marks you have learned.

A **Fill in each list below.**

Cat Names	City Names	Food Names
1. Buddy	1. _____	1. _____
2. _____	2. _____	2. _____
3. _____	3. _____	3. _____

B **Use your lists to write sentences.**

1. Write a **telling sentence** about three cats.

_____

_____

2. Write an **asking sentence** about three cities.

_____

_____

3. Write an **exciting sentence** about three foods.

_____

_____

C Write contractions for the words below.

1. did not _____ didn't _____

2. you are _____ you're _____

3. I am _____ I'm _____

4. it is _____ it's _____

5. they will _____ they'll _____

6. cannot _____ can't _____

7. we have _____ we've _____

8. has not _____ hasn't _____

9. is not _____ isn't _____

10. she is _____ she's _____

D Fill in each blank with a word that shows ownership.

1. The dog has a ball. It is the _____ dog's _____ ball.

2. Alisha has a computer. It is _____ Alisha's _____ computer.

3. Our teacher has a bike. It is our _____ teacher's _____ bike.

4. Barry has a pet bird. It is _____ Barry's _____ pet bird.

Name

_____

Capital Letters for Names and Titles

Use **capital letters** for people's names and titles.

title   **name**

Mr. Thomas lives in a little house.
Mrs. Thomas lives there, too.

A Add capital letters where they are needed. Cross out the lower-case letter you want to change. Write the correct capital letter above it.

1. Our class helper is mrs. cantu. → M C

2. The school nurse is mr. thomas. → M T

3. Yesterday, will and I went to see dr. paula. → W D P

4. I asked ms. demarko to read me a story. → M D

5. Mr. and mrs. chang picked us up at camp. → M C

6. Tomorrow, ms. banks and sally are coming over. → M B S

7. Our dentist is dr. villa. → D V

B Draw a picture or paste a photo of your favorite grown-up.

Write two sentences telling why you like this grown-up. Make sure to use the grown-up's title and name each time.

1. _____

   _____

2. _____

   _____

Name _____

Capital Letters for Days of the Week

Use **capital letters** for days of the week.

Sunday   **W**ednesday

A Answer the questions below. Remember to use capital letters correctly.

1. Which day comes after Saturday? _____Sunday_____

2. Which day is between Tuesday and Thursday?

_____Wednesday_____

3. Which day begins with the letter "F"? ____Friday____

4. Which day is the first day of the school week?

_____Monday_____

5. Which day comes after Friday? ____Saturday____

6. Which day is before Wednesday? ____Tuesday____

7. Which day comes before Friday? ____Thursday____

B Put the days of the week in the correct order, starting with Sunday.

Thursday   Sunday   Tuesday   Monday

Friday   Wednesday   Saturday

1. _Sunday_

2. _Monday_

3. _Tuesday_

4. _Wednesday_

5. _Thursday_

6. _Friday_

7. _Saturday_

Write a sentence about your favorite day of the week.

_____

_____

_____

Name _____

Capital Letters for Months of the Year 1

Use **capital letters** for the months of the year.

February   May

A **Use capital letters for the months in these sentences.**

1. The first day of spring is in ~~m~~arch.   M

2. The first day of summer is in june.   J

3. The first day of fall is in september.   S

4. The first day of winter is in december.   D

5. The first month of the year is january.   J

6. The shortest month is february.   F

7. Usually july and august are the hottest months.   J   A

8. april showers bring spring flowers.   A

B Here are three more months. Write each month correctly.

may _____ May _____

october _____ October _____

november _____ November _____

Write one sentence about each month above.

1. _____

_____

_____

2. _____

_____

_____

3. _____

_____

_____

Name _____

Capital Letters for Months of the Year 2

Use **capital letters** for the months of the year.

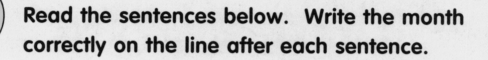

A Read the sentences below. Write the month correctly on the line after each sentence.

1. Handwriting Day is the 12th of january. _____January_____

2. Groundhog Day is in february. _____February_____

3. Arbor Day is in april. _____April_____

4. Memorial Day is the last Monday in may. _____May_____

5. My birthday is in june. _____June_____

6. Independence Day is the fourth of july. _____July_____

7. Labor Day is in september. _____September_____

8. Fire Prevention Week is during october. _____October_____

9. Thanksgiving Day is in november. _____November_____

B Unscramble these months and write them correctly on the lines below. Remember to use a capital letter for the first letter!

1. uejn   June

2. gsatuu   August

3. hamrc   March

4. yrjnuaa   January

5. larip   April

6. yma   May

7. tbreoco   October

8. eeedmbcr   December

9. eyfbarru   February

10. ljuy   July

11. ervbnome   November

12. tpbreesme   September

Name _____

Capital Letters for Holidays

Use **capital letters** for the names of holidays.

Father's **D**ay   **T**hanksgiving **D**ay

A Use capital letters for the holidays in these sentences. (*Day* is part of many holiday names.)

1. *N* *Y* *D*
   new year's day is in January.

2. We made cards for *V* valentine's *D* day.

3. We celebrate *P* presidents' *D* day in February.

4. *M* mother's *D* day and *M* memorial *D* day are always in May.

5. One holiday in June is *F* flag *D* day.

6. July 4 is *I* independence *D* day.

7. The first Monday in September is *L* labor *D* day.

8. The second Monday in October is *C* columbus *D* day.

B Write the names of three holidays found in the sentences on page 47.

1. _____

2. _____

3. _____

Now use the names of those three holidays in sentences.

1. _____

_____

_____

2. _____

_____

_____

3. _____

_____

Name

_____

Capital Letters for Names of Places

Use a **capital letter** for the name of a city, a state, or a country.

City	State	Country
Carson City	Nevada	France
Rome	Iowa	Chad

 **A** — **Write the city, state, or country correctly in the following sentences.**

1. *Make Way for Ducklings* takes place in the city of boston. _____Boston_____

2. The Everglades are in florida. _____Florida_____

3. My grandma is from ireland. _____Ireland_____

4. Mt. Fuji is in japan. _____Japan_____

5. The Sears Tower is in chicago. _____Chicago_____

6. The Peach State is georgia. _____Georgia_____

7. The capital of Alaska is juneau. _____Juneau_____

B Write the answers to the following questions. Use correct capitalization.

1. Which city or town do you live in?

_____

2. Which state do you live in?

_____

3. What is one state that is near your home state?

_____

4. What city does the President of the United States live in?

_____

5. What country were you born in?

_____

6. Which country would you most like to visit?

_____

Name

_____

Capital Letter for I

Use a **capital letter** for the word *I*.

↗ I have curly red hair.
Cory and I like to tap-dance.

A **Write the word I in each of these sentences.**

1. Jimmy and ___I___ are friends.

2. Sometimes ___I___ go to his house.

3. ___I___ ride there on my bike.

4. Sometimes Jimmy and ___I___ play at the park.

B **Write two sentences of your own using the word I.**

1. _____

_____

2. _____

_____

Draw a picture of yourself in the box below. Then write three sentences about yourself. Use the word *I* in each sentence.

1. _____

_____

2. _____

_____

3. _____

_____

Name

Capital Letters to Begin Sentences

Always use a **capital letter** for the first word in a sentence.

We go to the park in the summer.

A Begin each of the following sentences with a capital letter.

O
1. one day we had a picnic.

A
2. aunt Jill brought a big bowl of fruit salad.

G
3. grandma made lemonade and biscuits.

W
4. we had sub sandwiches and carrot sticks.

A
5. all the kids played softball before lunch.

A
6. after the game everyone drank lemonade.

G
7. grandma's biscuits were the best part of the picnic.

T
8. the ants liked the crumbs we dropped.

B Put a capital letter at the beginning of each sentence. Put a period at the end of each sentence.

there's a swimming pool at our park sometimes we go there for a swim i learned how to swim last year now I can go in the deep end of the pool my little sister can't swim yet she stays in the shallow end maybe I'll teach her how to swim

KEEP GOING

Write two sentences about things you like to do in the summer. Remember to use capital letters and periods.

1. _____

_____

2. _____

_____

3. _____

_____

Name

Capital Letter for a Speaker's First Word

Use a **capital letter** for a speaker's first word.

He asked, "Can you guess what this is?"

A **Add capital letters where they are needed.**

1. Our teacher asked, "do you know the story of the blind

men and the elephant?"

2. "i do," said Jasmine. "one man feels the elephant's

trunk. he thinks an elephant is like a big snake."

3. "another man feels the ear," Kerry added. "he thinks

an elephant is like a big fan."

4. Jasmine said, "another man feels the leg. he thinks an

elephant is like a tree trunk."

5. Then Ms. Tyler asked, "how could they know the truth?"

6. Kerry said, "they could work and talk together."

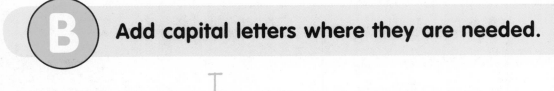

B Add capital letters where they are needed.

1. Ms. Tyler said, "T̶that's right, Kerry."

2. She asked, "W̶when do you like to work together?"

3. Kerry answered, "I̶i like working together to perform

plays."

4. Jasmine added, "T̶that's something one person can't

usually do alone."

Complete this sentence telling what the elephant thinks about the blind men.

The elephant said, "_____

_____."

Name _____

Capital Letters for Book Titles

Most words in book titles begin with **capital letters.**

↘ <u>Town Mouse, Country Mouse</u>

Some words do not begin with capital letters (unless they are the first or last word of a title). Here are some examples:

a   an   the   and   but   of
to   with   by   for   on

A   **Write the four underlined book titles correctly on the lines below.**

I went to the library yesterday. I found some wonderful books! I checked out <u>madison in new york</u>, <u>fishing with dad</u>, <u>hattie and the fox</u>, and <u>my brother needs a boa</u>.

1. <u>Madison in New York</u>

2. Fishing with Dad

3. Hattie and the Fox

4. My Brother Needs a Boa

B Write down the titles of your favorite book and magazine.

Book: _____

Magazine: _____

Write a note telling someone about your favorite book or magazine.

Dear_____ ,

_____

_____

_____

_____

_____

Your friend,

_____

Name

Capital Letters Review

This activity reviews some of the different ways to use **capital letters**.

A Put capital letters where they are needed.
(There are 19 in all.) Watch for these things:
* first word in a sentence,
* names and titles of people, and
* names of cities, states, and countries.

O
our class is studying rivers.   M B
mr. banks read a

book to us about the N nashua R river.   T the book was

written by L lynne C cherry.   W we also learned about the

N nile R river in A africa.   I it is the longest river in the

world.   M ms. J johnson visited our class.   S she went

down the A amazon R river on a raft!   S she showed

slides of her trip.

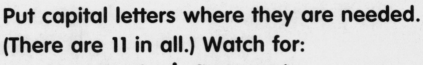

B Put capital letters where they are needed. (There are 11 in all.) Watch for:
* a speaker's first word.
* names of days and months.
* names of holidays.

1. Joel said, "<u>m</u>y favorite day is <u>s</u>unday. What's yours?"

2. "<u>s</u>unday is my favorite day, too," I answered.

3. "<u>w</u>hat's your favorite month?" Molly asked.

4. I said, "<u>m</u>y favorite month is <u>j</u>uly, because it's summer, and that's when I was born."

5. Molly said, "<u>m</u>y favorite month is <u>d</u>ecember, because that's when we celebrate <u>h</u>anukkah."

6. "<u>t</u>hat's when we celebrate <u>c</u>hristmas," I said.

C Put capital letters where they are needed in these titles.

1. <u>t</u>he <u>t</u>igger <u>m</u>ovie

2. <u>t</u>he <u>f</u>ox and the <u>h</u>ound

Name _____

Plurals

Plural means more than one. For most nouns, make the plurals by adding **-s**.

desk ➜ desk**s** window ➜ window**s**

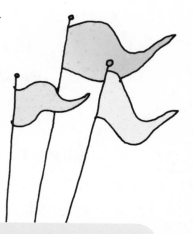

 A **Here is a list of things that may be in your classroom. Write the plural forms of the nouns. Then add two of your own examples.**

1. flag _____ flags _____

2. table _____ tables _____

3. eraser _____ erasers _____

4. pencil _____ pencils _____

5. book _____ books _____

6. marker _____ markers _____

7. door _____ doors _____

8. ruler _____ rulers _____

9. _____ _____

10. _____ _____

B **Fill in the blanks by changing the singular word under the line into a plural word.**

There are 16 _____girls_____ and 10 _____boys_____
                 (girl)   *(boy)*

in my class this year. We have one teacher and two

_____helpers_____ . There are three learning
(helper)

_____centers_____ in the classroom. In the reading center
(center)

there are lots of _____magazines_____ . The art center has
                    (magazine)

some very bright _____markers_____ . In the writing center
                (marker)

there's a whole box of _____pencils_____ and many different
                    (pencil)

_____kinds_____ of paper. I love my classroom!
(kind)

Write a sentence telling how many boys and girls there are in your class.

_____

_____

_____

Name _____

Plurals Using -s and -es 1

For most nouns, make the **plurals** by adding **-s**.

| one bird | two birds |
| a bike | four bikes |

For some nouns, you need to do more. Add **-es** to words that end in **sh, ch, s,** or **x**.

| a bush | some bushes |
| one box | two boxes |

 **A** **Write the plurals of the following nouns. It's easy—just add -s.**

1. bug   **bugs**

2. river   rivers

3. eye   eyes

4. ear   ears

5. sister   sisters

6. dog   dogs

7. house   houses

8. desk   desks

9. tree   trees

10. lake   lakes

B Make the following nouns plural. They all end in *sh*, *ch*, *s*, or *x*. You will need to add *-es*.

1. brush _____brushes_____   5. crash _____crashes_____

2. class _____classes_____   6. patch _____patches_____

3. bench _____benches_____   7. boss _____bosses_____

4. fax _____faxes_____   8. bunch _____bunches_____

C Fill in each blank with the correct plural. You will need to add *-s* to some nouns and *-es* to other nouns.

1. At the petting zoo there are baby _____lions_____
   (lion)

   and _____foxes_____ .
   (fox)

2. There are three _____hamsters_____ and
   (hamster)

   two _____gerbils_____ in my classroom.
   (gerbil)

3. My mom makes _____lunches_____ for me and
   (lunch)

   my two _____brothers_____ .
   (brother)

Name _____

Plurals Using
-s and -es 2

Make the **plurals** of most nouns by adding **-s**.

one snack   two snacks

For nouns that end in **sh**, **ch**, **s**, or **x**, add **-es** to make the plurals.

one lunch   two lunches

A   **Write the plurals of the following nouns. Add -s or -es.**

1. apple   ___apples___

2. carrot   ___carrots___

3. dish   ___dishes___

4. glass   ___glasses___

5. spoon   ___spoons___

6. box   ___boxes___

7. peach   ___peaches___

8. sandwich   ___sandwiches___

9. raisin   ___raisins___

10. fork   ___forks___

Draw a lunchbox on your own paper. Include some of the things you just listed.

Words That Change to Make Plurals

A few nouns make their **plurals** by changing letters and words. Here are some examples of irregular plurals.

child – children
foot – feet
goose – geese
man – men

mouse – mice
wife – wives
woman – women
wolf – wolves

A **Fill in each blank with the correct plural from the nouns above.**

1. There's a song about three blind _____ mice _____ .

2. You clap with your hands and walk with your _____ feet _____ .

3. Ducks and _____ geese _____ like to swim in ponds.

4. Sheep need to be protected from _____ wolves _____ .

5. Cartoons are for _____ children _____ , but_____ men _____

and _____ women _____ watch them, too.

6. Husbands have _____ wives _____ .

Name _____

Plurals of Words That End in *y* 1

Here are two rules for making **plurals** of nouns ending in *y*.

Rule 1   If there is a consonant right before the *y*, change the *y* to *i* and add *-es*.

one ba**b**y   two bab**ies**

Rule 2   If there is a vowel right before the *y*, just add *-s*.

one turk**e**y ➜ three turkey**s**

 A)   **Write the plurals of the following nouns. Use rule 1.**

1. cherry _____cherries_____

2. kitty _____kitties_____

3. party _____parties_____

4. berry _____berries_____

5. guppy _____guppies_____

6. bunny _____bunnies_____

7. pony _____ponies_____

8. puppy _____puppies_____

9. country _____countries_____

10. worry _____worries_____

B **Make the following nouns plural. Use rule 2 from page 69.**

1. monkey _____monkeys_____   **3.** toy _____toys_____

2. ray _____rays_____   **4.** holiday _____holidays_____

KEEP GOING

Circle three of the plurals you made on pages 69–70. Use each one in a sentence.

1. _____

_____

2. _____

_____

3. _____

_____

Name
_____

Plurals of Words That End in *y* 2

Here are two rules for making **plurals** of nouns ending in *y*.

Rule 1   If there is a consonant right before the *y*, change the *y* to *i* and add *-es*.

one ba**b**y   two bab**ies**

Rule 2   If there is a vowel right before the *y*, just add *-s*.

one turk**e**y   three turkey**s**

A   **Make the following nouns plural using rule 1 or rule 2.**

1. story   _____stories_____

2. diary   _____diaries_____

3. donkey   _____donkeys_____

4. key   _____keys_____

5. baby   _____babies_____

6. day   _____days_____

Write Source Page 315–317, 402, and 404

Plurals Review

This activity reviews making **plurals**.

A **Make these nouns plural by adding -s or -es.**

1. glass _____glasses_____
2. brush _____brushes_____
3. frog _____frogs_____

4. bus _____buses_____
5. dress _____dresses_____
6. worm _____worms_____

B **Make these nouns plural by adding -s or changing y to i and adding -es.**

1. monkey _____monkeys_____
2. puppy _____puppies_____
3. day _____days_____

4. turkey _____turkeys_____
5. toy _____toys_____
6. cherry _____cherries_____

C **Change these words to make them plural.**

1. mouse _____mice_____
2. foot _____feet_____

3. woman _____women_____
4. knife _____knives_____

Name

Abbreviations

Put a **period** after a person's title.
Mr. Mrs. Ms. Dr.

Ms • Walters   Mr • Johnson

A **Put periods after the people's titles in these sentences.**

1. Mr•Forest is our next-door neighbor.

2. Mr• and Mrs• Forest have a very big garden.

3. Mrs• Forest works in her garden on cool mornings.

4. Her friend Dr• Maynard stops to visit before work.

5. Mrs• Forest gives Dr• Maynard some pretty flowers
to take to the office.

6. After dinner, Mr• Forest likes to weed the garden.

7. Mrs• Forest helps him water the plants.

B Think of four people who work in your school.
Write their names below. Be sure to write Mr.,
Mrs., Ms., or Dr. before each.

1. _____

2. _____

3. _____

4. _____

Choose two of the people.
Write a sentence about each person.

1. _____

_____

2. _____

_____

Name _____

Abbreviations for Days and Months

When writing sentences, you should write the full names of the days and the months.

Today is Tuesday, October 9.

You should also know the **abbreviations** for the names of the days and the months.

Tuesday ➜ Tues.   October ➜ Oct.

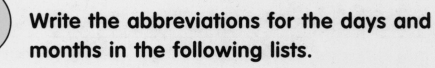

A **Write the abbreviations for the days and months in the following lists.**

1. Sunday _____Sun._____   **7.** February _____Feb._____

2. Friday _____Fri._____   **8.** March _____Mar._____

3. Wednesday _____Wed._____   **9.** November _____Nov._____

4. Thursday _____Thurs._____   **10.** August _____Aug._____

5. Saturday _____Sat._____   **11.** September _____Sept._____

6. Monday _____Mon._____   **12.** January _____Jan._____

Post Office Abbreviations

The US Postal Service suggests using all capital letters and no periods in abbreviations.

948 **N** LINCOLN
North

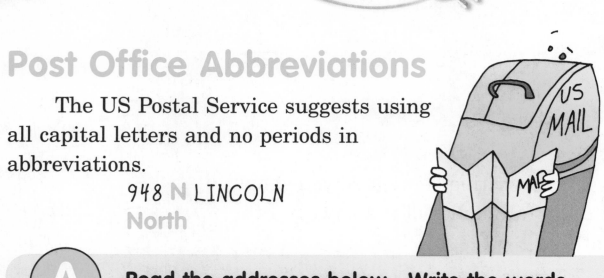

A — Read the addresses below. Write the words for the underlined abbreviations.

1. 1060 W ADDISON <u>ST</u>

_____Street_____

2. 1600 PENNSYLVANIA <u>AVE</u>

_____Avenue_____

3. 28 <u>E</u> 20TH ST

_____East_____

4. 7400 GRANT <u>RD</u>

_____Road_____

5. 413 <u>S</u> EIGHTH STREET

_____South_____

6. 40 PRESIDENTIAL <u>DR</u>

_____Drive_____

Name _____

Checking Mechanics Review 1

This activity reviews some of the ways to use capital letters.

A **Put capital letters where they are needed. There are 21 for you to find.**

D   T
dear theresa,

   H   H   F   T   M
   how are you? how is life in florida? today ms.

M   I
martinez said she wished we could all visit you. i

            I   J
told her i get to visit you in june!

   I   L   P   P   I
   i just read a book called lon po po. it is a

                        C   L
good story from china. lee gave me the book for my

birthday.

   M   J
   mrs. james said she hopes you like your new

            D
school. do you?

                              Your friend,

                              Roger

B Fill in the blanks below. Use your *Write Source* if you need help.

1. Write two days of the week that are school days:

   _____   _____

2. Write the name of a holiday: _____

3. Write your first name: _____

4. Write the name of a planet: _____

5. Write your teacher's name: _____

Now use the words you just wrote to complete this story.

It was _____ , but there was no school. It
         (day of the week)

was _____ . _____ had a busy
   (name of the holiday)   *(teacher's name)*

day planned. _____ was going to build a
         (your name)

spaceship and blast off to _____ .
         (planet)

Name
_____

Checking Mechanics Review 2

This activity reviews plurals and abbreviations.

A   **Write the plural of each animal name.**

1. cow _____cows_____

2. donkey _____donkeys_____

3. finch _____finches_____

4. goose _____geese_____

5. guppy _____guppies_____

6. mouse _____mice_____

7. fox _____foxes_____

8. pig _____pigs_____

9. puppy _____puppies_____

10. turkey _____turkeys_____

B   **Write the abbreviation for each day of the week.**

1. Monday _____Mon._____

2. Tuesday _____Tues._____

3. Wednesday _____Wed._____

4. Thursday _____Thurs._____

5. Friday _____Fri._____

6. Saturday _____Sat._____

7. Sunday _____Sun._____

C Write the abbreviations for the months of the year. Notice some months are not abbreviated.

1. January   _Jan._

2. February   _Feb._

3. March   _Mar._

4. April   _Apr._

5. May   _May_

6. June   _June_

7. July   _July_

8. August   _Aug._

9. September _Sept._

10. October   _Oct._

11. November _Nov._

12. December _Dec._

Name _____

Using the Right Word 1

Some words sound alike, but they have different spellings. They also have different meanings. These words are **homophones**. Here are some examples:

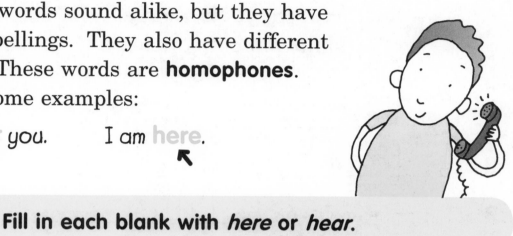

I hear you.   I am here.

A   **Fill in each blank with *here* or *hear*.**

1. I asked my dog Dan to come _____here_____ .

2. Can you _____hear_____ what I am saying?

3. Did you _____hear_____ what happened to Sara?

4. _____Here_____ is the ball I thought I lost.

5. I _____hear_____ music.

6. My dog can _____hear_____ better than people.

B   **Write a sentence using *hear* and *here*.**

_____

_____

C Read the example sentences using *no* and *know*. Then fill in each blank with the correct word.

Anna said, **"No** thanks."
I **know** about computers.

1. There is _____no_____ more soup.

2. I _____know_____ where to get some.

3. Just answer yes or _____no_____ .

4. Do you _____know_____ the new girl?

5. I don't _____know_____ her yet.

6. There is _____no_____ school tomorrow.

D Write a sentence using *no* and *know*.

_____

_____

Name _____

Using the Right Word 2

Some words sound alike, but they have different spellings. They also have different meanings. These words are **homophones**. Here are some examples:

These shoes are new.   I knew the answer.

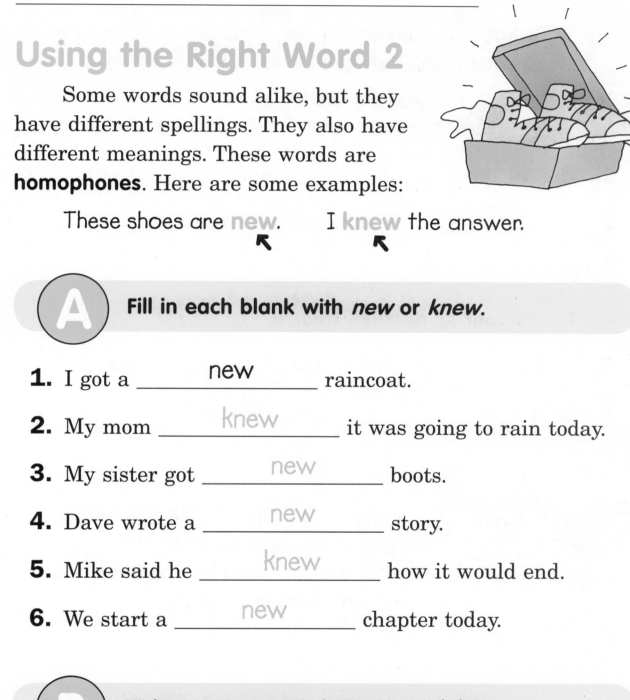

A   **Fill in each blank with *new* or *knew*.**

1. I got a _____ new _____ raincoat.

2. My mom _____ knew _____ it was going to rain today.

3. My sister got _____ new _____ boots.

4. Dave wrote a _____ new _____ story.

5. Mike said he _____ knew _____ how it would end.

6. We start a _____ new _____ chapter today.

B   **Write a sentence using *new* and *knew*.**

_____

_____

C Read the sentence using *its* and *it's*. Then fill in each blank with the correct word.

It's washing **its** kitten.

1. The cat uses ____its____ tongue.

2. ____It's____ washing the kitten's fur.

3. The kitten needs ____its____ mother.

4. The mother gives the kitten ____its____ food.

5. ____It's____ fun to watch the kitten grow.

6. Soon, ____its____ eyes will open!

Remember: If the words *it is* sound right in the sentence, use the contraction *it's*. Write a sentence for *its* and another using *it's*.

_____

_____

_____

Name _____

Using the Right Word 3

Some words sound alike, but they have different spellings. They also have different meanings. These words are **homophones**. Here are some examples:

I have two cats.
I have a dog, too.
I go to Pine Elementary.

A **Fill in each blank with *two*, *to*, or *too*.**
Too can mean "also" or "more than enough."

1. We are going _____ to _____ the beach.

2. We can only stay for _____ two _____ hours.

3. Can Marla come, _____ too _____ ?

4. I like to take a radio _____ to _____ the beach.

5. Just don't play it _____ too _____ loud.

B **Write a sentence using *two* and *to*.**

_____

_____

C Read the sentence using *one* and *won*. Then fill in each blank with the correct word.

One summer I **won** a ribbon.

1. There was _____ *one* _____ race.

2. I was so fast, I _____ *won* _____.

3. Mr. Wang gave me _____ *one* _____ blue ribbon.

4. I showed it to _____ *one* _____ of my cousins.

5. My mom couldn't believe I _____ *won* _____.

6. That was _____ *one* _____ great day.

D Write a sentence using *one* and *won*.

_____

_____

Name _____

Using the Right Word 4

Some words sound alike, but they have different spellings. They also have different meanings. These words are **homophones**. Here are some examples:

We saw *their* new puppy.
(*Their* shows ownership.)

There are three pets now.

They're lots of fun.
(*They're* = they are.)

A   **Fill in each blank with *their*, *there*, or *they're*.**

1. _____There_____ are four kids in the Clark family.

2. We play freeze tag in _____their_____ backyard.

3. _____They're_____ my next-door neighbors.

4. _____Their_____ mother loves animals.

5. Sometimes _____they're_____ busy feeding the pets.

6. _____There_____ are messes to clean up, too!

B Write three sentences using at least two of these words in each sentence: *their*, *there*, and *they're*.

1. _____

_____

2. _____

_____

3. _____

_____

C Draw a picture to match one of your sentences.

Name

Using the Right Word Review 1

This activity reviews the **homophones** you have practiced.

A **Write the correct word in each blank.**

1. Sam took _____two_____ rats _____to_____ school.
(two, to, too)   (two, to, too)

2. The white rat _____ate_____ the food.
(eight, ate)

3. Someone yelled, "Don't bring them in _____here_____!"
(hear, here)

4. Miss Green said, "I _____know_____ what to do."
(no, know)

5. The rats like to sleep in _____here_____ .
(hear, here)

6. I _____know_____ Sam likes his rats.
(no, know)

7. He has a pet spider, _____too_____ .
(two, to, too)

8. Don has a _____ new _____ pet parrot.
(new, knew)

9. _____ There _____ are more than 300 kinds of parrots.
(Their, There, They're)

10. Don will _____ buy _____ a book about parrots.
(buy, by)

11. Then he will _____ know _____ how to care for his pet.
(no, know)

12. You should _____ hear _____ the parrot talk!
(hear, here)

B Write three sentences. Use one of these words in each sentence: *to, two, too.*

1. _____

_____

2. _____

_____

3. _____

_____

Name

Using the Right Word Review 2

 Before each sentence is a group of words. Choose the correct word to fill in each blank.

1. **(hear, here)** "Did you _____hear_____ that Uncle Andy and

   Aunt Sue are coming _____here_____ ?" I asked.

2. **(know, no)** "Oh, _____no_____ , I didn't _____know_____

   that," Lea answered.

3. **(Ant, Aunt)** _____Aunt_____ Sue got a sailboat," I said. "She

   painted a red _____ant_____ on the side of the boat."

4. **(their, there, they're)** "I hope _____they're_____ bringing

   _____their_____ boat when they come," Lea said.

5. **(knew, new)** "Sure," I said. "They _____knew_____ we'd

   want to sail in the _____new_____ boat."

B Below are three homophone pairs. Pick one pair, and draw a picture showing those words. (Use *Write Source* if you need to check meanings.) Then write a sentence about your picture.

one won   blew blue   dear deer

_____

_____

_____

_____

Sentence Activities

This section includes activities related to basic sentence writing, kinds of sentences, and sentence problems. In addition, KEEP GOING, which is at the end of many activities, encourages follow-up practice of certain skills.

Name

_____

Understanding Sentences

A **sentence** tells a complete thought.

This is not a complete thought:
On the window.

This is a complete thought:
A bug is on the window.

 **Check whether each group of words is a complete thought or not.**

		Complete Thought	
		Yes	No
1.	From the downstairs music room.		✓
2.	The sound was very loud.	✓	
3.	Covered his ears.		✓
4.	After that.		✓
5.	He shut the front door.	✓	
6.	Max played the drums.	✓	
7.	Ming played the piano.	✓	
8.	Mom the silver flute.		✓

B **Fill in each blank with a word that completes the thought.**

1. _____ was playing with a ball.

2. The _____ rolled down the hill.

3. _____ ran after it.

4. Then a big, hairy _____ ran after it, too.

5. The _____ got the ball and kept running.

6. Was the _____ gone for good?

Draw a picture about sentence 4.

Name _____

Parts of a Sentence 1

Every **sentence** has two parts, the **subject** and the **predicate**. The subject is the naming part. The predicate tells what the subject is doing. It always includes the verb.

Joe **planted a seed.**
subject ↗   ↖ predicate

The dirt **covered the seed.**
subject ↗   ↖ predicate

A Underline the subject with one line. Underline the predicate with two lines.

1. Joe watered his seed every day.

2. He watched it carefully.

3. A leaf popped out.

4. The leaf grew larger.

5. A flower bloomed one morning.

6. Joe told his mom.

B **Write a verb for each sentence.**

1. Mom _____ bread.

2. I _____ her.

3. I _____ the flour.

4. I _____ the bowls.

5. Mom _____ the bread in the oven.

6. I always _____ the first slice of bread.

C **Check whether the underlined words are the subject or the predicate of the sentence.**

	Subject	Predicate
1. Your body <u>has a lot of bones</u>.		✓
2. <u>Your longest bone</u> is in your leg.	✓	
3. Your ribs <u>look like a cage</u>.		✓
4. Your smallest bone <u>is in your ear</u>.		✓
5. <u>Jellyfish</u> have no bones.	✓	
6. <u>A skeleton</u> is all bones.	✓	

© Great Source. All rights reserved.

Name _____

Parts of a Sentence 2

Every **sentence** has two parts, the **subject** and the **predicate**. The subject is the naming part. The predicate tells what the subject is doing. It always includes the verb.

<u>Haley</u> <u>came</u> to the party.

subject ↗   ↖ predicate

A   Fill in each blank with a word from the box. You may use some words more than once. These words are the subjects in your sentences.

Poems	**Ms. Day**	**Sam**	**Tacos**
Eddy	**Winter**	**Roses**	**Sarah**

(Answers will vary.)

1. _____ plays on the soccer team.

2. Last summer, _____ drove to Ohio.

3. _____ grow in Grandpa's garden.

4. _____ are my favorite food.

5. _____ sleeps in a tent.

B Fill in each blank with a verb from the box. You will use each word only once. Each verb will be included in the predicate part of the sentence.

learned	barked	is	went
hit	sang	eats	gave

1. Bobby ___hit___ a home run.

2. The dog ___barked___ loudly.

3. Steve ___eats___ toast every morning.

4. Our teacher ___gave___ us a test.

5. Kerry ___sang___ a song for the class.

6. At camp, Cheri ___learned___ to ride a horse.

7. My sister's name ___is___ Gail.

8. We all ___went___ for a hike yesterday.

Name

Kinds of Sentences 1

A **telling sentence** makes a statement. Put a period after a telling sentence.
Buster is out in the rain.

An **asking sentence** asks a question. Put a question mark after an asking sentence.
Where is Buster?

A — Write *T* before each telling sentence, and put a period after it. Write *A* before each asking sentence, and put a question mark after it.

___A___ **1.** What is Sandy doing?

___T___ **2.** Sandy is making a bird feeder.

___A___ **3.** Why is she doing that?

___T___ **4.** She wants to see what kinds of birds will come.

___A___ **5.** Where will she put the bird feeder?

___T___ **6.** She's going to hang it in a tree.

___A___ **7.** What kind of food will she put in it?

___T___ **8.** Sandy bought some birdseed for her feeder.

B Draw a picture of some birds at a bird feeder.

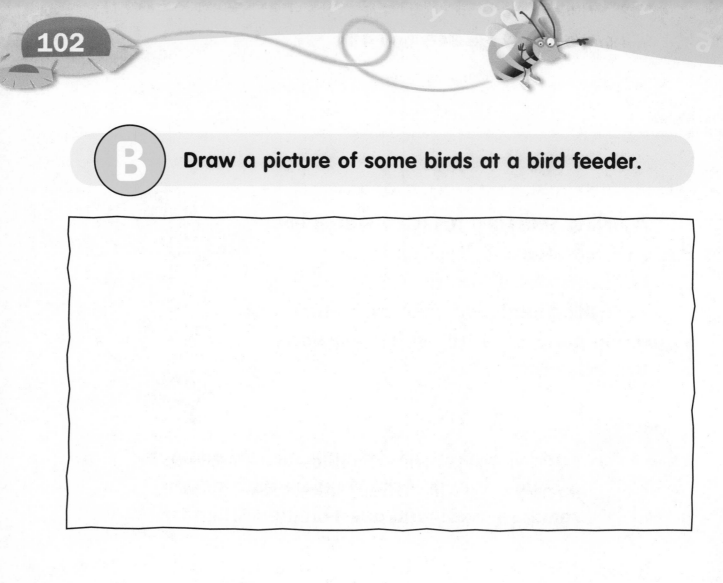

 Write one telling sentence and one asking sentence about your picture.

1. Telling Sentence: _____

_____

_____

2. Asking Sentence: _____

_____

_____

Name

Kinds of Sentences 2

A **telling sentence** makes a statement. Put a period after a telling sentence.
I'll feed Buster.

An **asking sentence** asks a question. Put a question mark after an asking sentence.
Would you feed Buster, please?

 Write a telling sentence that is an answer for each asking sentence. Make sure you write complete sentences.

(Answers will vary.)

1. What happened to your shoes?

_____

2. Who left the door open?

_____

3. How did you get all muddy?

_____

4. Have you read Too Many Tamales?

_____

B Pretend that you are only four years old. Write some asking sentences that a four-year-old might ask. Two examples have been done for you.

1. _Where do bugs come from?_

2. _Why does it get dark at night?_

3. _____

4. _____

5. _____

Pick two questions from above. Write telling sentences to answer them. (Write interesting answers that are complete sentences!)

1. _____

_____

2. _____

_____

Name _____

Sentence Review

This reviews what you have learned about sentences.

A **Write S after each sentence. Write X after each group of words that is not a sentence.**

1. My dad and I.   _X_

2. Went to Blue Hills Park.   _X_

3. We hiked to the top of a big hill.   _S_

4. Above the clouds!   _X_

5. Then Treasure Cave.   _X_

6. It was scary and dark inside.   _S_

7. Later, we saw three fat raccoons.   _S_

8. We had a lot of fun.   _S_

9. Will visit the park again.   _X_

B **Read page 339 in your *Write Source* to see how the writer made each group of words a complete thought.**

C Underline and label the subjects and the predicates in the sentences that begin with *I*. The first sentence has been done for you.

Dear Grandma,

                                   S   P   S   P

Guess what? I lost another tooth! I bit into an apple.

S   P

I feel the new hole in my mouth now.

                                             S

Mom will bring me to your house next week. I like

 P   S   P

your yard. I think your new slide is great!

Will you make smoothies for me? See you soon.

                     Love,

                     John

 **KEEP GOING** Copy one asking sentence and one telling sentence from the letter.

1. Telling Sentence:_____

_____

2. Asking Sentence:_____

_____

Language Activities

The activities in this section are related to the parts of speech. All of the activities have a page link to *Write Source*. In addition, KEEP GOING, which is at the end of many activities, encourages follow-up practice of certain skills.

Name

_____

Nouns

A **noun** names a person, a place, or a thing.

Person	**Place**	**Thing**
student	park	pizza
friend	mall	candle

A Write what each noun is: *person*, *place*, or *thing*. Add three nouns of your own.

1. firefighter   _____person_____

2. library   _____place_____

3. hammer   _____thing_____

4. teacher   _____person_____

5. pencil   _____thing_____

6. store   _____place_____

7. _____

8. _____

9. _____

B Write **N** if the word is a noun. Write **X** if the word is not a noun.

___N___ **1.** paper ___X___ **4.** bring ___X___ **7.** and

___X___ **2.** go ___N___ **5.** girl ___X___ **8.** hot

___N___ **3.** bee ___N___ **6.** store ___N___ **9.** kite

C Underline the noun in each sentence.

1. The <u>bus</u> is yellow.

2. The <u>spider</u> jumped.

3. This <u>game</u> is hard.

4. Look at the <u>duck</u>!

5. The <u>sky</u> looks pretty.

6. A <u>friend</u> called.

Write a sentence about your favorite toys. Then underline the nouns in your sentence.

_____

_____

_____

Name
_____

Common and Proper Nouns 1

A **common noun** names a person, place, or thing.
A **proper noun** names a special person, place, or thing.

Common Noun	Proper Noun
boy	Tony Prada
school	Hill Elementary
city	Lexington

A proper noun begins with a capital letter.
Some proper nouns are more than one word.

A   **Underline the common noun in each sentence.**

1. The <u>class</u> is busy writing.

2. Our <u>teacher</u> likes to help.

3. A <u>girl</u> is reading quietly.

4. The <u>street</u> is shiny and wet.

5. This sandy <u>beach</u> is hot.

6. Let's swim in the <u>pool</u>!

7. My <u>puppy</u> is furry and brown.

8. He has a red <u>collar</u>.

B   **Underline the proper noun in each sentence.**

1. We stopped at <u>Jefferson Library</u>.

2. <u>Susie</u> wanted a book about horses.

3. This book is about <u>President Lincoln</u>.

4. <u>Principal Brown</u> visited the library.

5. He speaks <u>Spanish</u>.

6. <u>Rosa Perez</u> does, too.

C   **Write *C* if the underlined word is a common noun. Write *P* if the underlined word is a proper noun.**

_C_   **1.** My neighbor walks her <u>dog</u> each afternoon.

_P_   **2.** My neighbor's name is <u>Mrs. Lee</u>.

_C_   **3.** Her dog likes <u>treats</u>.

_P_   **4.** <u>Alf</u> is a funny dog.

_C_   **5.** One day he got on a <u>bus</u>.

_C_   **6.** The bus <u>driver</u> said, "No dogs on the bus!"

Name

Common and Proper Nouns 2

A **common noun** names any person, place, or thing. A **proper noun** names a special person, place, or thing.

Common Noun	Proper Noun
holiday	New Year's Day
country	Mexico

A proper noun begins with a capital letter. Some proper nouns are more than one word.

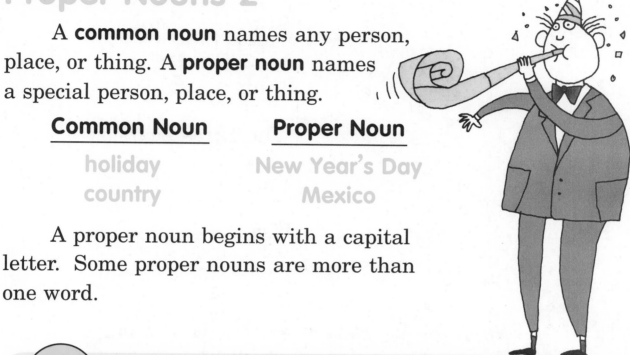

A Write *C* if the word is a common noun. Write *P* if the word is a proper noun.

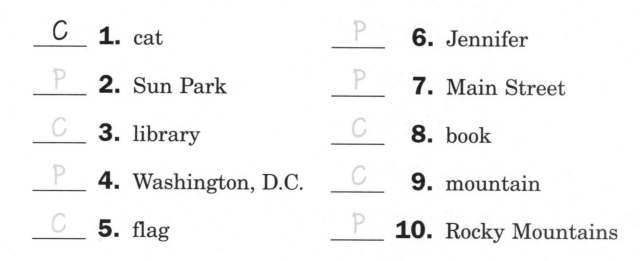

_C_ **1.** cat   _P_ **6.** Jennifer

_P_ **2.** Sun Park   _P_ **7.** Main Street

_C_ **3.** library   _C_ **8.** book

_P_ **4.** Washington, D.C.   _C_ **9.** mountain

_C_ **5.** flag   _P_ **10.** Rocky Mountains

B Draw a line from each common noun to the proper noun that fits with it.

1. girl   United States

2. boy   Fluffy

3. cat   "The Three Bears"

4. country   Tom

5. story   Lisa

C Write *C* if the underlined noun is a common noun. Write *P* if the underlined noun is a proper noun.

_P_ 1. Today is <u>Christmas</u>!

_C_ 2. There is no <u>school</u> today.

_C_ 3. The <u>air</u> is freezing cold.

_P_ 4. <u>Aunt Lizzie</u> visited us.

_C_ 5. Kevin brought <u>popcorn</u>.

_P_ 6. Chin is from <u>Korea</u>.

Name
_____

Singular and Plural Nouns

Singular means one.

elephant

Plural means more than one.
elephants

Plural nouns usually end with **s**.

A Write **S** if the noun is singular. Write **P** if the noun is plural.

__P__ **1.** boxes   __S__ **4.** rug

__S__ **2.** table   __S__ **5.** truck

__P__ **3.** chairs   __P__ **6.** toys

B Write **S** if the underlined noun is singular.
Write **P** if the underlined noun is plural.

__S__ **1.** I like <u>art</u>.   __P__ **3.** <u>Paints</u> are messy.

__P__ **2.** I have <u>crayons</u>.   __S__ **4.** It's for my <u>sister</u>.

C Underline the plural noun in each sentence.

1. The cow has black and white spots.

2. Some piglets are pink.

3. Potatoes spilled out of the grocery bag.

4. My sister baked dinner rolls yesterday.

5. Tony took off his muddy shoes.

6. Erin held the tiny kittens.

KEEP GOING

Draw a picture about one of the plural nouns you underlined. Write the noun under your picture.

Name

Possessive Nouns

A **possessive noun** shows ownership.
A possessive noun has an **apostrophe**.

Tia's toy boat was left out in the yard.
(The toy boat belongs to Tia.)

After the storm, we found it in the dog's house.
(The house belongs to the dog.)

A **Circle the possessive nouns.**

1. (Mike's) story about Mr. Bug was fun to read.

2. Mr. (Bug's) house was flooded when it rained.

3. Mr. (Bug's) family hopped in a toy boat.

4. All the little Bugs waited for the (storm's) end.

5. Finally, the boat floated to a (dog's) house.

6. The (dog's) name was Buddy.

7. The little Bugs asked if they could share their new

(friend's) home.

8. The (story's) title is "The Bugs Find a Buddy."

B Draw a picture of one of these things from the story:

* Mr. Bug's flooded house.
* the child's toy boat.
* the dog's house.

KEEP GOING

Write a sentence telling about your picture. Use a possessive noun. (Remember to use an apostrophe.)

_____

_____

Name

Pronouns 1

A **pronoun** is a word that takes the place of a noun.

Noun	**Pronoun**
Todd did it.	He did it.
Sally laughed.	She laughed.
The rope broke.	It broke.
The skates are too big.	They are too big.

  Circle the pronouns that replace the underlined nouns in the sentences below.

1. <u>Holly</u> gave Katy a Mexican coin.

(She) gave Katy a Mexican coin.

2. Katy put the <u>coin</u> in a safe place.

Katy put (it) in a safe place.

3. <u>Peggy and Jo</u> wanted to see the coin.

(They) wanted to see the coin.

4. Then <u>Jay</u> asked to see it, too.

Then (he) asked to see it, too.

B Draw a line from each noun to the pronoun that could replace it.

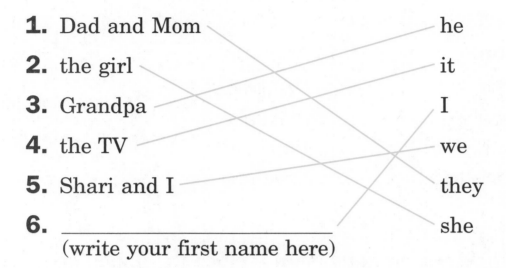

1. Dad and Mom   he
2. the girl   it
3. Grandpa   I
4. the TV   we
5. Shari and I   they
6. _____ she
   (write your first name here)

C In each sentence, write a pronoun to replace the noun. If you need help, check the list of pronouns on page 320 in *Write Source*.

1. _____They_____ went to a movie.
   (Jim and Ray)

2. _____He_____ broke his arm.
   (The boy)

3. A doctor fixed _____it_____ .
   (the arm)

4. _____She_____ is a good writer.
   (Jane)

Name

Pronouns 2

A **pronoun** can take the place of a possessive noun. A possessive noun shows ownership.

Noun	**Pronoun**
Jan's bicycle	her bicycle
Dave's skateboard	his skateboard
the bird's wing	its wing
Mike and Laura's poem	their poem

A Circle the pronouns that take the place of the underlined nouns in the sentences below.

1. Juanita's coat is red.

(Her) coat is hanging up.

2. At the picnic, Jake's lunch fell into the water.

(His) lunch was soggy.

3. Yesterday Sam and Sarah missed the bus.

(Their) bus left early.

4. The dog was very excited.

(It) chewed on a big bone.

B Underline the pronoun in each sentence. Draw a picture of the pet rat.

1. Here is <u>my</u> pet rat.

2. Dad likes <u>its</u> pink ears.

3. Mom likes <u>its</u> long tail.

4. Bogart is <u>our</u> favorite pet.

5. <u>He</u> has red eyes.

6. Ted pets <u>his</u> white fur.

7. <u>We</u> bought a blue cage.

C Draw a line to the pronoun that could replace the underlined words.

1. I heard <u>Tim and Judy's</u> song.   ours

2. I know <u>your sister's</u> name.   Its

3. Here comes <u>Ricky's</u> friend.   their

4. <u>The book's</u> cover got wet.   his

5. The tree house is <u>yours and mine</u>.   her

Name _____

Pronouns 3

A **pronoun** is a word that takes the place of a noun.

Jason made a sandwich.
Then he ate it.
(The pronouns *he* and *it* take the place of the nouns *Jason* and *sandwich*.)

 A **Fill in each blank with a pronoun that replaces the underlined word or words.**

1. Joe and Ann read a poem. ___They___ read it aloud.

2. Tanya drew a map. ___She___ showed it to me.

3. My brother and I have a clubhouse. ___We___ made it ourselves.

4. I hope you're coming to my party. ___It___ will be fun.

5. Mom heard our music. ___It___ was too loud.

6. Tony is coming over. ___He___ is my friend.

7. The monkeys ate bananas. ___They___ were hungry.

8. This book is great. ___It___ has good pictures, too.

B Use each pronoun in a sentence.

I	we	she	they

1. _____

2. _____

3. _____

4. _____

C Draw a picture to go with one of your sentences.

Name

Action Verbs

There are different kinds of **verbs**.
Some verbs show action:

Mom found our jump rope.
She gave it to us.

A Underline the action verb in each sentence.

1. Al brings the jump rope.

2. Eli and Linda hold the rope.

3. They twirl the rope.

4. The other kids count.

5. Scott's dog barks at the children.

6. Today Al jumps 100 times!

7. Then Linda takes a turn.

8. Mother waves from the window.

9. The kids laugh.

B Here are some more action verbs. Fill in each blank with a verb from this box.

dive	hear	pop
roars	visit	eat

1. Paul and Ann _____visit_____ the zoo.

2. They _____hear_____ some lions.

3. One of the lions _____roars_____ at them.

4. The elephants _____eat_____ lots of peanuts.

5. The polar bears _____dive_____ into the pool.

6. Prairie dogs _____pop_____ out of their tunnels.

KEEP GOING

Write a sentence about the zoo. Use an action verb.

_____

_____

_____

Name

Action and Linking Verbs

Action verbs show action. Here are some examples:

kick   tell   throw   ask   run   write

Linking verbs complete a thought or an idea. Here are some examples:

am   was   is   were   are   be

A   **Write _A_ if the underlined verb is an action verb. Write _L_ if the verb is a linking verb.**

___A___ **1.** Soccer players <u>kick</u> the ball.

___A___ **2.** Football players <u>throw</u> the ball.

___L___ **3.** I <u>am</u> cold.

___A___ **4.** Pat and Rob <u>run</u> around the track.

___L___ **5.** She <u>is</u> a fast runner.

___L___ **6.** They <u>are</u> both in second grade.

___A___ **7.** He <u>paints</u> pictures.

___L___ **8.** Pete and Joni <u>were</u> sick.

B Pick five action verbs from the list on page 444 in *Write Source*. Use each action verb in a sentence.

1. _____

_____

2. _____

_____

3. _____

_____

4. _____

_____

5. _____

_____

KEEP GOING

Write a sentence using the linking verb *am*.

_____

_____

Name

_____

Verbs: Present and Past Tense

A verb that tells what is happening now is called a **present-tense verb**.

Sean is in second grade.
He takes swimming lessons every week.

A verb that tells what happened in the past is called a **past-tense verb**.

Last year he was in first grade.
He learned to play soccer.

A Check whether each underlined verb is in the present tense or the past tense.

	Present Tense	Past Tense
1. Bobby <u>broke</u> his leg last weekend.		✓
2. He <u>fell</u> out of a big tree.		✓
3. Now he <u>has</u> a cast on his leg.	✓	
4. He <u>is</u> home from school this week.	✓	
5. Yesterday I <u>took</u> him his homework.		✓
6. I <u>wrote</u> my name on his cast.		✓
7. Bobby <u>walks</u> with crutches.	✓	

B Complete the following sentences. Write the present-tense verb or the past-tense verb in the blank. The first one has been done for you.

Present Tense

1. Now Mom _____makes_____ my lunches for school.
   (makes, made)

2. Now I _____am_____ eight years old.
   (am, was)

3. The sidewalk _____gets_____ slippery when it snows.
   (gets, got)

4. Now Stanis _____takes_____ swimming lessons.
   (takes, took)

Past Tense

1. Last week I _____walked_____ to school with Hector.
   (walk, walked)

2. Yesterday Lydia _____wrote_____ a letter to her aunt.
   (write, wrote)

3. Last summer our family _____went_____ camping.
   (goes, went)

4. This morning I _____was_____ late for school.
   (am, was)

Name

Irregular Verbs

Irregular verbs do not follow the same rules as other verbs. They change in different ways.

	Present tense	Past tense
Example:	Birds fly.	Birds flew.

Study the irregular verbs in your textbook. Then complete the exercise below.

A Circle the correct verb in each sentence.

1. My friend Kara (*rode,* *ridden*) a pony.

2. Uncle Billy (*came,* *come*) to visit us.

3. Last night, I (*sung,* *sang*) with my cousin.

4. Alfonso (*saw,* *seen*) a moose at the zoo.

5. Oscar (*done,* *did*) a good job on his art project.

6. The pitcher (*threw,* *throw*) the ball to first base.

B In the sentences below, fill in the blank with the correct form of the verb shown.

1. was   am

present: I ____am____ taking dance lessons.

past: I started dancing when I ____was____ four.

2. hide   hid

present: Sometimes, I ____hide____ from my dog.

past: Yesterday, I ____hid____ from him.

3. ran   run

present: We ____run____ with my big brother.

past: Last week, we ____ran____ at the track.

4. knew   know

present: I ____know____ Olivia.

past: When we met, I ____knew____ we would be friends.

Name _____

Adjectives 1

An **adjective** describes a noun or a pronoun. An adjective often comes before the word it describes.

Megan has long hair.
Randy wears a black cap.

Sometimes an **adjective** comes after the word it describes.

Parrots are colorful.

A Underline the adjective that describes each circled noun.

1. Elephants are <u>huge</u> (animals.)

2. Their (skin) is <u>wrinkled</u>.

3. Their <u>ivory</u> (tusks) are <u>long</u> (teeth.)

4. Elephants use their <u>floppy</u> (ears) as <u>giant</u> (fans.)

5. An elephant's trunk works as a <u>useful</u> (tool.)

6. It can pick up <u>small</u> (peanuts.)

7. A <u>cool</u> (river) is an elephant's <u>favorite</u> (place.)

B Fill in each blank with an adjective that describes the circled noun.

(Answers will vary.)

1. Elephants make _____ noises.

2. Elephants have _____ trunks.

3. They have _____ feet.

4. Elephants can carry _____ loads.

5. Would you take a _____ ride on an

elephant?

6. How would you get on a _____ elephant?

C Underline each adjective that describes the circled pronoun.

1. You are smart.

2. He is funny.

3. They look tired.

4. I am hungry.

5. It is green.

6. We are cold.

7. She feels sick.

8. They taste stale.

Name _____

Adjectives 2

An **adjective** describes a noun or a pronoun. An adjective often comes before the word it describes.

The hungry bear sniffed the berries.

Sometimes an **adjective** comes after the word it describes.

The bear was hungry.

  Underline the adjectives in this story. There are 14 in all. (Don't underline *a* or *that*.)

Once there was a little brown bear.

In the cool forest, she ate crunchy roots and red berries.

She drank from a clear stream.

Fish swam by the little bear.

On summer days, the bear ate and ate.

In the fall, little bear changed.

She was a great, big bear.

She crawled into a cozy den for a long winter nap.

B Write one more sentence for the story about the little bear. Underline the adjectives you use.

_____

_____

C Write two sentences using adjectives from the box below. Try using more than one adjective in your sentences.

hairy	purple	loud	cold
windy	wet	sweet	soft
chewy	sleepy	strong	sour

1. _____

_____

2. _____

_____

Name
_____

Articles

The words **a**, **an**, and **the** are **articles**.

Use **a** before a consonant sound.

a kite

Use **an** before a vowel sound.

an ocean

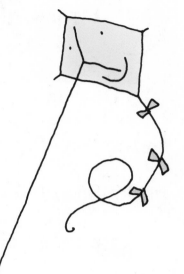

A **Write *a* or *an* before the following words.**

_____an_____ **1.** attic

_____a_____ **2.** chicken

_____a_____ **3.** shovel

_____an_____ **4.** elephant

_____a_____ **5.** tooth

_____a_____ **6.** giant

_____a_____ **7.** dinosaur

_____an_____ **8.** apple

_____a_____ **9.** spider

_____a_____ **10.** whale

_____a_____ **11.** shadow

_____an_____ **12.** envelope

_____an_____ **13.** idea

_____a_____ **14.** monkey

_____an_____ **15.** orange

_____a_____ **16.** package

_____a_____ **17.** kettle

_____an_____ **18.** inchworm

B **Fill in the word *a* or *an* in the spaces below.**

One day ____a____ spider with yellow feet climbed

to the top of ____a____ slide. The slide was in ____a____

park. Soon the spider heard ____a____ radio playing her

favorite song. The song was ____an____ old tune called

"The Eensy Weensy Spider." The spider began to tap her

eight yellow feet. ____An____ inchworm heard the music,

too. He inched his way over to the slide and began to tap

all of his feet. What ____a____ funny sight to see!

____A____ spider and ____an____ inchworm were dancing in

the park.

**Draw a picture of the spider and
the inchworm. Add a new sentence to
your picture.**

Name _____

Adjectives that Compare

Adjectives use different word endings to make comparisons. The ending **-er** compares two people, places or things. The ending **-est** compares three or more.

Compare **two**:
> My brother's room is smaller than my room.

Compare **three or more**:
> The baby's room is the smallest room in our house.

A **Fill in each blank with the correct form of the adjective.**

long, longer, longest

1. A grass snake is ___long___ .

2. A boa is ___longer___ than a grass snake.

3. A python is the ___longest___ snake in the zoo.

funny, funnier, funniest

1. Garrett's riddle was ___funny___ .

2. Leah's riddle was ___funnier___ than Garrett's riddle.

3. Ty's riddle was the ___funniest___ one in class.

B Circle the adjective that compares two people, places, or things. Underline the adjective that compares three or more.

1. Kenny is the tallest player on the team.

2. Silver Lake is deeper than Cross Creek.

C Write one sentence using the first adjective. Then, write another sentence using the second adjective.

bigger

(Anwers will vary.)

_____

_____

happiest

_____

_____

Name

Adverbs

An **adverb** is a word that describes a verb. It tells *when,* *where,* or *how* an action is done.

Some adverbs tell **when:**

yesterday   soon   always   early

Some adverbs tell **where:**

here   inside   up   below

Some adverbs tell **how:**

quietly   carefully   loudly   quickly

 **In each sentence below, circle the adverb that tells *when*.**

1. Aldo has never seen snow.

2. We woke up early so we could go fishing.

3. Tomorrow, our class is going to the museum.

4. Salma always wears her hair in braids.

B In each sentence below, fill in the blank with an adverb that tells *where*.

(Answers will vary.)

1. Our teacher will be _____ tomorrow.

2. Do you want to play _____ this afternoon?

3. I saw a mouse run _____ the stairs!

C Fill in each blank with an adverb from the box below. These adverb tells *how*.

(Answers will vary.)

gently	quickly	softly	cheerfully

1. Alexis smiled *cheerfully* _____ when she won the race.

2. "Have you seen Cory?" I asked *softly* _____.

3. Malik danced *quickly* _____ as he sang.

4. I rocked my baby sister *gently* _____.

Name

Prepositions

A **preposition** is used to add information to a sentence.

Toby hit the ball over the fence.

Ally put a quarter in her bank.

Here are some common prepositions.

onto	up	with	at	of
before	below	like	in	to
as	over	down	along	on

 A **Circle the prepositions in the paragraph below. The chart above will help you.**

Troy left camp (before) breakfast. 2. He pushed his bike (to) the top (of) the hill. 3. Soon, he was racing (down) it. 4. The wind rushed (through) his hair. 5. The bike's wheels bumped (along) the grassy path. 6. "Woo-hoo!" Troy shouted (with) joy.

B Use the prepositions in this box to complete the following sentences. You will use one of the prepositions twice.

like	of	in	above	until

1. Beluga whales live ___in___ cold, Arctic waters.

2. Belugas are gray ___until___ they become adults.

3. Then they turn white ___like___ their parents.

4. They are often called "sea canaries" because ___of___ their songs and chatter.

5. Belugas swim ___in___ groups called pods.

6. Their sounds can be heard ___above___ the water.

C Write a sentence including a preposition from the box above.

_____

_____

_____

Name

_____

Conjunctions

A **conjunction** connects words or groups of words. The words *and* and *but* are the most common conjunctions.

Ramon writes poems and sings songs.

I was on time, but Tom wasn't there.

 **Write one sentence using the conjunction *and*.**

_____

_____

 **Write one sentence using the conjunction *but*.**

_____

_____

Conjunctions

Two other conjunctions that connect words or groups of words are *or* and *so*.

Is Todd **or** Jaimee ready to bat?

It looked like rain, **so** she brought an umbrella.

 C **Read the story below, and circle the seven conjunctions.**

The Tortoise (and) the Hare

Who won the race, the tortoise (or) the hare? They started out together, (but) the hare was much faster. He was way ahead of the tortoise, (so) he took a nap. The hare was snoring (and) dreaming when the tortoise walked by. Soon, the hare woke up, (and) he was amazed at what he saw. The tortoise was near the finish line! The hare ran to catch up, (but) it was too late. The tortoise won the race.

Name

Interjections

An **interjection** shows excitement.
Some common interjections are:

Wow!   Yum!   Help!

Ouch!   Oops!   Hey!

A **Write interjections to complete these sentences.**

(Answers will vary.)

1. _____ ! This soup tastes delicious.

2. _____ ! I dropped my slice of pizza.

3. _____ ! I'm falling off the swing.

B **Write a sentence using one of the interjections from above.**

(Answers will vary.)

_____

_____

C Draw a picture for each sentence below. Label each picture with an interjection.

(Answers willl vary.)

_____
(interjection)

Look what I can do.

_____
(interjection)

That bug is huge.

_____
(interjection)

I pinched my finger!

_____
(interjection)

I dropped my lunch tray.

Name _____

Parts of Speech Review 1

In this activity, you will review the parts of speech you have practiced: **noun (N), pronoun (P), verb (V),** and **adjective (A)**.

 **What part of speech is underlined in each sentence? Write *N, P, V,* or *A* in the blank.**

___A___ **1.** I like <u>toasted</u> cheese sandwiches.

___V___ **2.** They <u>smell</u> buttery and <u>look</u> golden brown.

___V___ **3.** When I <u>bite</u> into one, I <u>see</u> the melted cheese.

___N___ **4.** Toasted cheese <u>sandwiches</u> taste crunchy on the outside and creamy in the middle.

___P___ **5.** <u>My</u> mom makes them on the griddle.

___P___ **6.** <u>I</u> could eat one every day!

___N___ **7.** I hope we have toasted cheese sandwiches for <u>dinner</u> tonight.

___A___ **8.** It would be a <u>super</u> way to end my day.

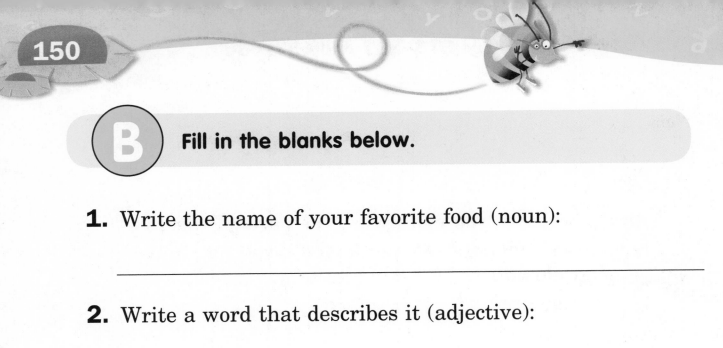

B Fill in the blanks below.

1. Write the name of your favorite food (noun):

_____

2. Write a word that describes it (adjective):

_____

C Fill in each blank with a word that is the correct part of speech.

1. _____ likes tuna sandwiches.
     (noun)

2. _____ like tacos better.
     (pronoun)

3. I _____ two tacos every day.
     (verb)

4. I like them with _____ cheese.
             (adjective)

5. Sandra's mom _____ the best tacos.
             (verb)

6. She puts _____ sauce on them.
         (adjective)

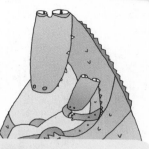

Name

Parts of Speech Review 2

A Use the adjectives and adverbs in the box below to fill in the blanks in the sentences. Use each word only once.

small	smaller	smallest	tallest
exciting	large	wild	

1. Our zoo is an ___exciting___ place to visit.

2. Many ___wild___ animals live there.

3. Some are ___large___ and others are ___small___.

4. The giraffe is the zoo's ___tallest___ animal.

5. Otters and beavers are ___smaller___ animals.

6. Chipmunks are the ___smallest___ animals at the zoo.

B **Underline the prepositions in these sentences.**

1. One cat rested <u>on</u> the desktop.

2. Another cat hid <u>inside</u> a drawer.

3. It hid <u>under</u> some papers.

C **Use a comma and a conjunction to combine these short sentences. Use _or, and,_ or _but_.**

1. Should we play inside? Should we play outside?

_____

2. We went to the park. We had a picnic.

_____

D **Write a sentence. Use one of the interjections below.**

Wow! **Yippee!** **Help!**

_____

_____